FORERUNNERS: IDEAS FIRST
FROM THE UNIVERSITY OF MINNESOTA PRESS

Original e-works to spark new scholarship

FORERUNNERS: IDEAS FIRST is a thought-in-process series of breakthrough digital publications. Written between fresh ideas and finished books, Forerunners draws on scholarly work initiated in notable blogs, social media, conference plenaries, journal articles, and the synergy of academic exchange. This is gray literature publishing: where intense thinking, change, and speculation take place in scholarship.

Ian Bogost
The Geek's Chihuahua: Living with Apple

John Hartigan
Aesop's Anthropology: A Multispecies Approach

Reinhold Martin
Mediators: Aesthetics, Politics, and the City

Shannon Mattern
Deep Mapping the Media City

Jussi Parikka
The Anthrobscene

Steven Shaviro
No Speed Limit: Three Essays on Accelerationism

THE GEEK'S CHIHUAHUA

The Geek's Chihuahua

Living with Apple

IAN BOGOST

University of Minnesota Press

Minneapolis

An earlier version of chapter 4 appeared as "The iPhones of Fall," *The Atlantic,* September 12, 2013. An earlier version of chapter 5 appeared as "The Cigarette of this Century," *The Atlantic,* June 6, 2012. An earlier version of chapter 6 appeared as "Hyperemployment, or the Exhausting Work of the Technology User," *The Atlantic,* November 8, 2013. A portion of chapter 8 appeared as "Yo," *The Atlantic,* June 19, 2014. An earlier version of chapter 9 appeared as "The End of the Hangup," *The Atlantic,* March 15, 2013. Chapter 10 previously appeared in *The Atlantic,* September 16, 2014.

Published by the University of Minnesota Press
111 Third Avenue South, Suite 290
Minneapolis, MN 55401-2520
http://www.upress.umn.edu

The University of Minnesota is an equal-opportunity educator and employer.

Contents

The Geek's Chihuahua

THINK BACK TO 2007, when you got the first iPhone. (You did get one, didn't you? Of course you did.) You don't need me to remind you that it was a shiny object of impressive design, slick in hand and light in pocket. Its screen was bright and its many animations produced endless, silent "oohs" even as they became quickly familiar. Accelerometer-triggered rotations, cell tower triangulations (the first model didn't have GPS yet), and seamless cellular/WiFi data transitions invoked strong levels of welcome magic. These were all novelties once, and not that long ago.

What you probably don't remember: that first iPhone was also terrible. Practically unusable, really, for the ordinary barrage of phone calls, text messages, mobile email, and web browsing that earlier smartphones had made portable. And not for the reasons we feared before getting our hands on one—typing without tactile feedback wasn't as hard to get used to as BlackBerry and Treo road warriors had feared, even if it still required a deliberate transition from T9 or mini-keyboard devices—but rather because the device software was pushing the limits of what affordable hardware could handle at the time.

Applications loaded incredibly slowly. Pulling up a number or composing an email by contact name was best begun before ordering a latte or watering a urinal to account for the ensuing delay. Cellular telephone reception was far inferior to other devices available at the time, and regaining a lost signal frequently required an antenna or power cycle. Wireless data reception was poor and slow, and the device's ability to handle passing in and out of what coverage it might find was limited. Tasks interrupted by coverage losses, such as email sends in progress, frequently failed completely.

The software was barebones. There was no App Store in those early days, making the iPhone's operating system a self-contained affair, a ladleful of Apple-apportioned software gruel, the same for everyone. That it worked at all was a miracle, but our expectations had been set high by decades of complex, adept desktop software. By comparison, the iPhone's apps were barebones. The Mail application, for example, borrowed none of its desktop cousin's elegant color-coded, threaded summary view but instead demanded inexplicable click-touches back and forward from folder to folder, mailbox to mailbox.

Some of these defects have been long since remedied in the many iterations of the device that have appeared since its 2007 debut. Telephony works well, and who uses the phone anymore anyway? Data speed and reliability have been updated both on wireless network infrastructures and in the smartphone itself. But other issues persist. For those who cut their computing teeth on desktops and laptops—the things that we used to mean when we used the word *computer*—manipulating mobile software still feels awkward and laborious. Those many taps of the original Mail app haven't been altered or remedied so much as they have become standardized. Now, we use all software in the convoluted manner mobile operating systems demand, from email to word processing to video editing.

But to issue complaints about usability misses the point of the iPhone, even all those years ago, and certainly today. The iPhone was never a device one should have expected to "just work," to quote Apple's familiar advertising lingo. It is a device one has to accommodate. It taught us how to tolerate Apple making us tolerate it. It put us in our place before Apple. This was the purpose of the iPhone, and this is its primary legacy.

Then, as now, the iPhone demands to be touched just right, in precisely the right spot on menu, list, or keyboard, and with precisely the right gesture. Likewise, it demands not to be touched just after, when being pocketed or moved or simply turned to place at one's ear. Doing otherwise erroneously launches, or quits, or selects, or deletes, or slides, or invokes Siri the supposedly intelligent personal assistant, or performs some other action, desired or not, slickly coupled to a touch or gestural control.

The iPhone resists usability, a term reserved for apparatuses humans make their servants. An iPhone is not a computer. It is a living creature, one filled with caprice and vagary like a brilliant artist, like a beautiful woman, like a difficult executive. Whether it is usable is not the point. To use the iPhone is to submit to it. Not to its interfaces, but to the ambiguity of its interpretation of them. To under-stand it as an Other, an alien being boasting ineffable prom-ise and allure. Touch here? Stroke there? Stop here? Do it again? The impressive fragility of the device only reinforces this sense—to do it wrong by dropping or misgesturing might lead to unknown consequences. Unlike other porta-ble devices—a Walkman or a traditional mobile phone—the iPhone embraces fragility rather than ruggedness. It demands to be treated with kid gloves. Even before you've first touched it, you can already hear yourself apologizing for your own blunders in its presence, as if you are there to serve it rather than it you. The iPhone is a device that can send you far out of your way, and yet you feel good about it. It is a device that can endear you to it by resisting your demands rather than surrendering to them.

Rather than thinking of the iPhone as a smartphone, like a Treo or a BlackBerry or, eventually, the Android devices that would mimic it, one would do better to think of the iPhone as a pet. It is the toy dog of mobile devices, a crea-ture one holds gently and pets carefully, never sure whether it might nuzzle or bite. Like a Chihuahua, it rides along with you, in arm or in purse or in pocket, peering out to assert both your status as its owner and its mastery over you as empress. And like a toy dog, it reserves the right never to do the same thing a second time, even given the same triggers. Its foibles and eccentricities demand far greater effort than its more stoic smartphone cousins, but in so doing, it chal-lenges you to make sense of it.

The BlackBerry's simplicity and effectiveness yielded a constant barrage of new things to do. And eventually, so would the smartphone—social media feeds and status updates replaced work with play-as-work, with *hyperemployment*, a term I'll explain soon enough. But that first iPhone resisted utility old and new. It acclimated us to the new quirks of touchscreen life, of attempting to accomplish complex tasks that would have been easy on a normal computer but laborious on a tiny screen that ran one program at a time. Today we've acclimated, accepting these inefficiencies as givens. But such an eventuality was never guaranteed, and iPhone had to train us to tolerate them. Like the infirm must endure physical therapy to reform damaged limbs and tissues, so the smartphone user needed to be trained to accept and overcome the intrinsic incapacities of the handheld computer.

This was harder than it sounds in retrospect. That first iPhone receded into itself at times, offering its owner no choice but to pet it in vain, or to pack it away it until it regained composure, or to reboot it in the hopes that what once worked might do so again. It was a beast of its vicissitudes. And it still is, albeit in different ways. To own an iPhone is to embrace such fickleness rather than to lament it in the hope for succor via software update. And even when one does come, it only introduces new quirks to replace the old ones: the slowdowns of an operating system upgrade launched to execute planned obsolescence, say, or via new sensors, panels, controls, and interfaces that render a once modernist simplicity baroque.

Indeed, when you would meet new iPhone users, they would share much more in common with smug, tired pet owners than with mobile busybodies. "Here, let me show you," one would say proudly when asked how she liked it. Fingers would stretch gently over photos, zooming and turning. They'd flick nonchalantly through web pages and music playlists. As with the toy dog or the kitten, when the iPhone fails to perform as expected, its owners would simply shrug in capitulation. "Who knows what goes through its head," one might rationalize, as she might do just the same when her Maltese jerks from sleep and scurries frantically, sliding across wood around a corner.

The brilliance of the iPhone is not how intuitive or powerful or useful it is—for really it is none of these things. Rather, the brilliance of the iPhone is in its ability to transcend the world of gadgetry and enter another one: the world of companionship. But unlike the Chihuahua or the bichon or even the kitten, the iPhone has no gender bias. It need not signal overwrought Hollywood glam, high-maintenance upper-class leisure, or sensitive loner solitude. iPhone owners can feel assured in their masculinity or femininity equally as they stroke and snuggle their pet devices, fearing no reprisal for fopishness or dorkship.

The Aibo and Pleo, those semirealistic robotic pets of the pre-iPhone era that attempted to simulate the form and movement of a furry biological pet, failed precisely because they did nothing else other than pretend to be real pets. The iPhone got it right: a pet is not an animal at all. A pet is a creature that responds meaningfully to touch and voice and closeness, but only sometimes. At other times, it retreats inextricably into its own mind, gears spinning in whatever alien way they must for other creatures. A pet is a sentient alien that cultures an attachment that might remain—that probably remains—unrequited. A pet is a bottomless pit for affect and devotion, yet one whose own feelings can never be truly known.

The iPhone offers an excuse to dampen the smartphone's obsession with labor, productivity, progress, and efficiency with the touching, demented weirdness that comes with companionship. Despite its ability to text, to tweet, to Facebook, to Instagram, perhaps the real social promise of iPhone lies elsewhere: as a part of a more ordinary, more natural ecology of real social interaction. The messy sort that resists formalization in software form. The kind that makes unreasonable demands and yet sometimes surprises.

And of course, the kind that overheats and flips into mania. Mania, it turns out, is what iPhone wants most. To turn us all into the digital equivalent of the toy dog–toting socialite obsessive or the crazy cat lady, doting and tapping, swiping and cooing at glass rectangles with abandon.

This is a book about some of that mania, and where it might be taking us.

What Is an App?

IN 2010, the American Dialect Society named *app* the word of the year. In announcing this dubious honor, the organization offered this abrupt definition of the term:

App (n)—The shortened slang term for a computer or smart phone application.

Even the American Dialect Society may not have realized how accurately it elucidated the matter. It's not just the term that's shortened, and it's not just the term that's slanged. It's also the *application itself* that's shortened and slanged in an app.

An app is an application—that old, staid term for a unit of executable computer software—smashed into bits. "The primary thing that Apple did," the game developer Steven An writes, "was create and market the concept of the 'app' as a $1–5 unit. They're doing to software what they did to music: they broke it up into little pieces and then gave consumers a nice place to shop for the pieces." The days of the software office suite have given way to a new era of individual software chunks, each purpose-built for a specific function. Or just as often, for no function at all.

And there's the rub of the new era of apps. The software suite may have been an authoritarian regime, with a few large companies offering a few top-down visions of how to use computers productively. But like the LP record, it told a coherent story—or at least it presented a complete aesthetic. Apps shatter the very idea of aesthetic coherence, turning computers into weird samplers that betray the smooth, slick exteriors of the devices that contain them. It's no accident that these gadgets also refuse the multitasking and deep integration of traditional graphical computer operating systems in favor of the fickle, one-thing-at-a-time attention of digital pets. Multitasking may have been omitted from early app-focused devices like the iPhone because of limited hardware resources, but it's evolved to become anathema to the app aesthetic. Apps are meant to be isolated from one another.

The architecture of iOS, the operating system that runs Apple's iDevices, even endorses isolation in its design. Despite their apparent power, iPhones and iPads have always been underpowered compared to desktop and laptop computers. The first iPhone included 128MB of random access memory (RAM), the data storage a computer uses to hold information for running applications. By the time multitasking came to iOS 4 in 2010, the devices meant to run it still only sported between 256MB and 512MB of RAM (Apple's MacBook laptops at that time shipped standard with 4GB of RAM). Multitasking, a software engineering term for running multiple processes at once, really referred to memory residence—the operating system would keep as many programs running as it could, until memory limitations forced a "background" app to close to accommodate requests from a "foreground" app.

It might be more accurate to call this practice "latertasking" instead of multitasking. Rather than putting apps away entirely, iOS keeps them close but inactive. As a result, the usage patterns we learned from the era of the graphical user interface (GUI) have shifted. Instead of moving rapidly between multiple applications on a windowed desktop, apps demand deliberate one-step-at-a-time action. Smartphones make latertasking palatable by making it necessary—there's just not enough screen real estate nor input methods to carry out multiple interactions at once. And so what once would have been a smooth transition from file manager to photo editor to layout program on the desktop becomes a staccatoed dance of taps and gestures and home button depressions, closing and opening whole programs, moving files to cloud storage just to reopen them a moment later somewhere else. It's the GUI interaction model exploded into shrapnel.

Ironically, the broken-into-bits model for software productivity is among the oldest around. UNIX, the server operating system first developed at Bell Labs in the late 1960s, features a modular design that encourages users to use (and program) small, focused programs that can direct input and output to one another. A data access program might direct its output into a processing program, which might in turn channel its output to a formatter for print display.

Both Apple's OS X desktop operating system and the simplified version of it that became iOS are based on versions of UNIX, but this low-level app-to-app interaction is largely unavailable, hidden by the gloss of the GUI and its promise of user-friendliness. Later versions of iOS offer a minimal version of app-to-app data piping, but only as tightly controlled by the operating system—sending images from Photos to Twitter, for example. The return to the tiny, purpose-built app is not a return to free-form, brick-by-brick computational productivity and creativity but the creation of a dense tenement block of isolated programs forced into submission by an absentee landlord.

The app is a mixed blessing for computer aesthetics, just like sampling is for music. On one hand, we get many variations of the same thing that can surprise us when refashioned in different permutations. But on the other hand, we get fewer coherent, complete takes. And there's a risk that deep meaning slowly seeps out of every unit as each does less and less. Apps and their cousins, isolated web services like Foursquare and Facebook, give us a preview of this potential future agony, one in which the most basic chunk of meaning is the conveyance of a piece of data from a database to a screen and back again. Here's where I was and here's what I looked like when I was there.

Critics will respond that apps allow people rather than corporations to define what's interesting or important to them, individuals synthesizing the configuration and use of apps like teenagers fashioning mix tapes. There's both truth and gloom in this observation. As exhilarating and rousing as that feeling might be, it's precious and fragile too. Apps are lithe and delicate and charming, but with that frivolous delight comes temporariness. If the baroqueness and oppression of applications are akin to the complexity of prog rock, then the lightness and simplicity of apps are akin to the carefree buoyancy of radio pop. Shortening and slang are easy and comfortable. They make you feel good. But soon enough, their freshness fades, and something else must come along to replace them. As in language, slang in software implies constant novelty. An app is software that's here, for a moment, and then gone.

3

Pascal Spoken Here

"HEAR HOW TOMMY WENT from knowing nothing about code to building one of Time's 50 Best Websites." So reads ad copy from Codecademy, one of many online, self-paced tools for learning to write software. Whether online or in institutions, "learn to code" has become the lazy mantra of today's educational aspiration.

Lost in debates about whether and how to learn to code is the fact that learning to program has become *harder* rather than easier, even as the personal computer has become more prevalent and influential. Issues of access and diversity notwithstanding, in the early days of the microcomputer, many of us learned to program because that's what one did with a personal computer. It sounds unlikely today, I know, but advertisements from the early days of the PC drive this point home. Consider a two-page spread from 1977, the first year of the Apple II. It ran in *Scientific American*, among other publications.

On the verso, a turtlenecked man sits at the kitchen table, working on some kind of chart portrayed nonchalantly on the display to his side. The gendered stereotype of the male

computer programmer–operator is unfortunately reinforced by the woman who stands at the sink in the background, but the implication is clear: computing is a kind of work that one can do at home—that one might *need* to do there.

On the recto, comprehensive ad copy flanks detailed specifications, including a glamour shot of the motherboard instead of the casing. "But you don't even need to know a RAM from a ROM to use and enjoy Apple II," the text reads. "It's the first personal computer with a fast version of BASIC—the English-like programming language—permanently built in. That means you can begin running your Apple II the first evening, entering your own instructions and watching them work, even if you've had no previous computer experience."

The implication is clear: you're going to bring home your new $1,298 Apple II, set it up on your kitchen table, and start writing some programs. And not just because you're a dork who reads *Scientific American*; no, the ad continues to explain that everyone in your house can learn to do it:

> But the biggest benefit—no matter how you use Apple II—is that you and your family increase familiarity with the computer itself. The more you experiment with it, the more you discover about its potential.

What's more, the ad suggests an organic oscillation between using the computer and programming it, the one influencing the other:

> Start by playing PONG. Then invent your own games using the input keyboard, game paddles and built-in speaker. As you

experiment you'll acquire new programming skills which will open up new ways to use your Apple II. You'll learn to "paint" dazzling color displays using the unique color graphics commands in Apple BASIC, and write programs to create beautiful kaleidoscopic designs. As you master Apple BASIC, you'll be able to organize, index and store data on household finances, income tax, recipes, and record collections. You can learn to chart your biorhythms, balance your checking account, even control your home environment.

Finally, there's a clear implication that becoming more fluent in computing involves becoming a more agile and determined programmer, not merely a more adept user:

> Best of all, Apple II is designed to grow with you. As your skill and experience with computing increase, you may want to add new Apple peripherals. For example, a refined, more sophisticated BASIC language is being developed for advanced scientific and mathematical applications. And in addition to the built-in audio, video and game interfaces, there's room for eight plug-in options such as a prototyping board for experimenting with interfaces to other equipment.

Another, undated ad targets educators, presumably for institutional purchases. It too depicts programming as an inevitable rather than a possible use of the machine: "Apple engages student interest with sound and color video. In fact, your students will be able to write programs and create high-resolution graphics." Later on, the ad expresses a sentiment almost entirely alien from the perspective of Apple in the twenty-first century. Instead of assuming that a computer is a device for consuming media, including software programs as apps, the educator's Apple II reprises the 1977

ad's implication that programming is an inevitable consequence of owning a computer:

> Once you've unlocked the power of the desk-top computer, you'll be using Apple in ways you never dreamed of. You don't want to be limited by the availability of pre-programmed cartridges. You'll want a computer, like Apple, that you can also program yourself. . . . The more you and your students learn about computers, the more your imagination will demand. So you'll want a computer that can grow with you as your skills and experience grow.

This copy underscores many of the differences between computing in the late 1970s and early 1980s and computing today. For one part, a computer was an investment, more like an appliance than a consumable. Like a pet of a different sort, in fact: a fixture in the home for work and for play that would remain a companion as indefinitely as its mortality would allow. The Apple II was unique in its facility for user expansion and customization in both software and hardware. But for another part, straight out of the box, anyone could make the computer do *something*. And then, soon enough, anyone with a little patience and interest could make the computer do *anything* it was capable of.

So fundamental was programming to the experience of computing that it even found its way into the advertising itself. A 1979 print ad promotes the availability of a Pascal development environment for the Apple II. It's is an amazing spread, partly because it includes a reverse-printed, iron-on decal that would produce a T-shirt with the message "Pascal Spoken Here." But the ad also makes good on the promise made in the 1977 "Introducing Apple II" ad by offering more advanced tools to help improve an owner's ability to program the machine:

> With Pascal, programs can be written, debugged and executed in just one-third the time required for equivalent BASIC programs. With just one-third the memory. On top of that, Pascal is easy to understand, elegant and able to handle advanced applications. It allows one programmer to pick up where another left off with minimal chance of foul up.

The mention of foul-ups conjures those lovely yet horrifying BASIC magazine listings, one of the standard ways to distribute and share programs at the time. Pascal, as it happens, went on to become the native development environment for the Apple Lisa and the original Macintosh. It was still possible to program the Mac in Object Pascal through System 6 and 7, and Apple supported the language up until the IBM PowerPC architecture switch in 1994.

These examples underscore the good fortune that blessed those of us who started using computers at or near the start of the microcomputer era. Learning a new language or environment was a far less frequent and more specific affair, and yet a far more familiar and comfortable one. Why? Because it was possible to learn to program computers in time with their very evolution.

When we advocate for "learning to code" today, we fail to remember that contexts like those of the era of the Apple II no longer exist. The problem is not just that coding has become more complex and more difficult, as common wisdom surrounding the "genius coder" might suggest. Rather, the machines themselves have changed. Once, not so long ago even, they were devices meant to be customized and added onto by their users, who were all assumed to be latent, potential programmers, much the way woodworkers were (and still are) expected to fashion jigs for their table saws, with their table saws. But today, computers are not just devices for everyone but devices *meant to be sold* to everyone.

Perhaps it was inevitable that computer users would lose touch with the process of crafting software as their ranks swelled from the thousands to the millions to the billions. But it's equally possible that the architecture, construction, marketing, and use of computers have contributed just as much to the decline of computational literacy among the computer user, in favor of the young, spry specialist.

In some cases, the weird, accidental material conditions of the practice of software development have an impact on the sort of practice it facilitates. For example, the separations created by long compiles in the days of applications (rather than apps) created invitations to dig deep into the design and operation of a programming language to avoid unnecessary delays and failures due to compilation errors. And before the Internet, programming environments were both better and more centrally documented, in print volumes or secondary texts that could be studied away from the computer.

Today, documentation is often renounced in favor of "crowdsourced" solutions, such as the coding help forums at Stackoverflow.com, a website where programmers can ask questions of one another and answer them. On one hand,

Apple lets you get personal with Pascal.

There's only one logical way to find out what a person wants in a personal computer.

Ask the person who'll be using one.

At Apple, we've been very successful at identifying just what people look for in computers. And then providing them with it.

In spades.

For serious enthusiasts, this means making available sophisticated innovations that are often conspicuously absent from other personal computers.

Like Pascal.

Apple II is one of the few personal computers that has it. And when you turn this

page and feast your eyes on the many advantages this high level, general-purpose language has to offer, you'll see why that's very good news indeed.

When you've got it, flaunt it.

If you'd like to let the world know who speaks Pascal, here's how:

Preheat iron (dry-wool setting) for 3 minutes. Slip garment on ironing board over scrap material. Remove wrinkles. Position transfer face down and pin edges to ironing board cover. Iron transfer slowly for one minute. If paper browns, iron is too hot. Let transfer cool for one minute, then unpin and slowly pull transfer straight up. Results are best when t-shirt is at least 50% polyester.

Pascal by the package.

Our high-level, full feature Language System consists of a plug-in 16K RAM language card, five diskettes containing Pascal as well as Integer BASIC and Applesoft extended BASIC, plus seven manuals documenting the three languages.

The beauty of this Language System is that it speeds up execution and helps cut unwieldy software development jobs down to size. Also, because the languages are on diskette, loaded into RAM, you can quickly and economically take advantage of upgrades and new languages as they're introduced.

Apple's Pascal language takes full advantage of Apple high resolution and color graphics, analog input and sound generation capabilities. It turns the Apple into the lowest priced, highest powered Pascal system on the market. With Pascal, programs can be written, debugged and executed in just one-third the time required for equivalent BASIC programs. With just one-third the memory.

On top of that, Pascal is easy to understand, elegant and able to handle advanced applications. It allows one programmer to pick up where another left off with minimal chance of foul up.

And, because Apple uses the UCSD Pascal standard, you're guaranteed to get the most comprehensive version available—and one that can be used on any computer that runs Pascal, no matter what the size. Which is really something an enthusiast can get enthused about.

To be more specific.

The Apple II's specs are tempting enough without the Language System and Pascal. With them, they're downright irresistible.

The text, normally displayed as 24 lines of 40 characters each, expands to 80 characters thanks to the use of horizontal scrolling.

Characters are normal, inverse or flashing, 5 x 7, upper case. Full cursor control is standard.

Since Pascal runs on an Apple computer with 48K bytes of on-board RAM, the additional 16K bytes on the language card bring the total to a full 64K bytes.

And, Pascal runs on the new Apple II Plus. It features an Auto-Start ROM that boots the Disk II at power-on for turn-key operation. Applesoft extended BASIC is resident in ROM.

Standard color graphics offer 40h x 48v resolution, or 40h x 40v with 4 lines text, in fifteen colors.

Black/white high resolution, bit-mapped graphics display 8K bytes of memory as a 280h x 192v image (140h x 192v in six colors).

Peripheral board connectors are fully buffered with interrupt and DMA priority structure.

And finally, since it weighs a mere 11 lbs. and has its own travel case, as an option, not only is it easy to get carried away with an Apple, it's easy to carry one away.

We've got your numbers.

800-538-9696. (In California, 800-662-9238.) Or write us at 10260 Bandley Drive, Cupertino, California 95014. When you contact us, we'll give you the name, address and telephone number of the Apple computer dealer nearest you.

If you'd like more information on the advantages of owning an Apple personal computer, he can fill you in. Personally.

many more people are available to assist with programming challenges. On the other hand, one already has to possess so much literacy to address those challenges that access is restricted rather than expanded. Back in the early 1980s, when a computer like the Apple IIe came with a BASIC manual, the beginning programmer at least found himself safely ensconced within the sandbox of a well-documented yet still powerful system. Today, computers are glass and aluminum mysteries off of whose surfaces computational curiosity slips like mercury.

I don't mean to invoke nostalgia for better, simpler times. Rather, to acknowledge that the deliberate or accidental conditions for creativity have an influence on the ways we carry out those practices. Ironically, as computers have become more popular and more diverse, as "learning to code" has become more desirable and marketable, the diversity of those practices may have declined more than proliferated.

When Apple moved to the App Store model for software distribution, it also introduced a submission and approval process for developers seeking to publish their apps. In addition to charging a ninety-nine-dollar annual fee just for the privilege of using the system, Apple's approval process— every app for sale gets vetted by the company—has proven arbitrary at best and questionable at worst. For example, Apple has a tendency to deny publication to politically controversial apps. (Among them is Molleindustria's 2011 title Phone Story, a mobile game about the political consequences of mobile electronics manufacture, among them Congolese coltan mining and Chinese electronics factory labor.) But another restriction imposed by Apple's centralization of publishing and distribution relates to the tools with which software is created in the first place.

Apple has always tested for and denied its publication of apps that use "private" application programming interfaces (APIs)—that is, programs that make use of portions of the operating system that Apple has created for internal use only. But at one point, Apple also attempted restrictions that dictated the programming languages and environments that could be used to write software for iOS:

> Applications must be originally written in Objective-C, C, C++, or JavaScript as executed by the iPhone OS WebKit engine, and only code written in C, C++, and Objective-C may compile and directly link against the Documented APIs (e.g., Applications that link to Documented APIs through an intermediary translation or compatibility layer or tool are prohibited).

The policy prevented apps from running interpreted code—that is, from loading and running software *within* an app. Emulators for older computers, such as the Commodore 64 and (ironically) the Apple II, were prohibited, as was the children's educational programming environment Scratch.

But it seems to have been launched as a frontal assault in Steve Jobs's unlikely war against Adobe's Flash tool kit, the cross-platform animation and programming environment first made popular on the Web in the 1990s. Adobe had created a Flash exporter for iPhone, which they scrapped in the wake of the prohibition, only to later reinstate it after the dust cleared. The Federal Trade Commission and the Department of Justice reportedly considered launching an antitrust investigation into Apple to determine if the policy would unlawfully foreclose competition on rival platforms—an unthinkable outcome in 1980, even if the Apple II was as successful then, relatively speaking, as the iPhone was thirty years later.

The computational ecosystem is burgeoning. We have more platforms today than ever before, from mobile devices to microcomputers to game consoles to specialized embedded systems. Yet, a prevailing attitude about computational creativity longs for uniformity: game engines that target multiple platforms to produce the same plain-vanilla experience; authoring tools that export to every popular device at the lowest common denominator; and, of course, the tyranny of the Web, where everything that once worked well on a particular platform is remade to work poorly everywhere (just think of Google Docs, which took Microsoft's bloated desktop office suite and refashioned its components into terrible online renditions). After Apple's prohibition of nonnative development tools, Flash developers responded with understandable fury. But rather than antitrust idealism, ignorance probably motivated their anxiety: many such developers just didn't possess an adeptness with iOS-native tools like Objective-C, and they feared being locked out of Apple's popular platform.

From our vantage point, Apple's 1977 version of learning and deploying programming might seem quaint, even if also appealing. Today we have offloaded such facilities into concepts like "hacker" and "maker," lifestyle activities that already imply that one has managed to "learn to code" by other means, and in which the act of programming or designing circuits becomes an end practiced for its own sake, often as an affectation.

But it is not entirely impossible to imagine recuperating such a situation, one in which hardware ships with the tools to make software for it—for personal use as much as for producing the latest hit app or billion-dollar start-up. Apple itself made gestures toward such a possible future in 2014, when it introduced a new programming language called Swift, meant to make iOS and OS X programming easier and more rapid. Still, programming has become so decoupled from computer ownership and use that a new language is hardly sufficient to return us to those salad days of the late 1970s. Back then, owning a computer entailed being a programmer, much like owning a sewing machine entailed being a seamster or a seamstress.

4

The Phones of Fall

WHEN APPLE LAUNCHED THE IPHONE 4 in 2010, the company's website featured large images of the device with the slogan "This changes everything. Again." Change has been a constant refrain in Apple's marketing over the years. The famous 1984 Macintosh ads—"Why 1984 won't be like 1984"—framed the computer as an agent of revolution. And the "Think Different" ads of the 1990s implied that purchasing one of Apple's underdog machines put you in the same company as other misunderstood genius underdogs. But "change" goes back further than that, too. Ads for the Apple II and the business-oriented Apple III in the early 1980s compared their power to that of famous inventors of ages past, including Henry Ford, Thomas Jefferson, and Ben Franklin, among others.

If you rewatch the original 2007 iPhone announcement, you'll be hard-pressed to deny the device's revolutionary claims have largely come to pass. But the "change" associated with subsequent models has been fairly modest, despite Apple's frequent claims to the contrary, among them the explicit mention in the iPhone 4's marketing motto. The

Edison had over 1,800 patents in his name, but you can be just as inventive with an Apple.

Apple is the company with the brightest ideas in hardware and software *and* the best support — so you can be as creative with a personal computer system as Edison was with the incandescent bulb.

How Apple grows with you.

With Apple's reliable product family, the possibilities of creating your own system are endless. Have expansion capabilities of 4 or 8 accessory slots with your choice of system.

Expand memory to 64K bytes or 128K bytes. Add an A to D conversion board. Plug into time sharing, news and electronic mail services. Use an IEEE 488 bus to monitor lab instruments. Add 4 or 6 disk drives — the 5¼", 143K bytes, high-speed, low-cost drive that's the most popular on the market.

Apple speaks many languages.

Since more than 100 companies create software for Apple, you'll have the most extensive library in the personal computer world. Want to write your own programs? Apple is fluent in BASIC, Pascal, FORTRAN, PILOT and 6502 assembly language.

There's even a series of utility programs called the DOS Tool Kit that not only lets you design high-resolution graphic displays, but lets you work wonders with creative animation.

More illuminating experiences in store.

You won't want to miss all the Apple products being introduced at your computer store all the time. Don't let history pass you by. Visit your nearest Apple dealer or call **800-538-9696**. In California, **800-662-9238**. Or write: Apple Computer, 10260 Bandley Drive, Cupertino, CA 95014.

apple computer inc.

CIRCLE NO. 9 ON FREE INFORMATION CARD

many generations of iPhone (we're up to six, as I write) hardly compare to the Apple II, the Macintosh, or even the original iPhone in their implications and impact. They have offered small but important updates: high-resolution displays, more sensors, increased battery capacity, faster processors, better cameras. Fingerprint security in iPhone 5s offered an interesting advance, but it's hardly an innovation akin to the printing press or the airplane or the personal computer. Indeed, it's not an innovation at all but merely a refinement and systematic rollout of an old idea that hadn't yet caught on but was just about ready to do so.

Why does Apple try to pass off a predictable (and increasingly easily predicted), gradual evolution of its existing platform as change of the more revolutionary kind? Hyperbole is one possible answer. "Change" has become an idea so synonymous with Apple that it must be perpetuated through its branding and marketing, even when real change may be lacking. Another might be hubris. In his push to get products done just his way, Steve Jobs had to create desire rather than satisfy need. And so "change" became the promise of every Apple product, even the earliest ones. Just take a look at the print ad for the 1983 Apple Lisa. It uses the same sentence construction as the iPhone 4 spread did in 2010: "This changes everything. Again." It even boasted the same full stop after "Again."

But neither of those explanations is complex or subtle enough to characterize Apple's approach to consumer electronics product launches. Change is no longer political nor social nor industrial, as in the case of 1984 or Henry Ford. Instead, it's commercial and aesthetic. For Apple, "change"

no longer refers to revolution. It refers to fashion. Apple is becoming more like Prada and less like Edison.

This has been the case for some time, it was just harder to notice as the iPhone was undergoing large-scale adoption. But in retrospect, Steve Jobs's keynotes functioned more like catwalks than like product demos. And the Apple Store has always been a boutique as much as an electronics shop.

But now that Jobs is gone, we can see this shift from futurism to fashion more clearly. Apple's head industrial designer, Jony Ive, has become its most prominent public figurehead, despite his shyness. Its products, too, look more like couture first, with computing to follow. Instead of promising change and revolution, the iPhone 5c offered itself "For the colorful," a slogan we'd be more likely to see from Benetton or J. Crew than from Apple. The company (maybe we should start calling it a "label") is releasing a new line, seasonally, and needs to train its audience to feel increasingly comfortable dropping hundreds of dollars each season. The "change" in question is not regime change but a change between tennis at the club and dinner downtown.

For its part, The iPhone 5s dispensed with the false promise of revolution in favor of the modest and sensible slogan "Forward thinking." The device's black, silver, and gold colors signal the elegance and simplicity we associate with choosing a finish for a Mercedes or a bezel for a watch. This design points even further into Apple's future than did the iPhone 5c's affordable couture seasonality: like an automobile, the top-end iPhone is becoming a necessity, even if a luxury one. Even the wealthy don't buy a new car every year. But when needed or strongly desired, a new model helpfully designates itself, along with a set of modestly novel features and styling choices that will be replaced soon enough. Hip fashion and elegant necessity aren't revolutionary, and it's dishonest to pretend they are. The Apple Watch, for its part, offers variations sure to compete in allure (and, at many thousands of dollars for the gold edition version) with the most prized of handmade Swiss timepieces. A wristwatch is many things, but a novelty it is not.

By 2014's introduction of the otherwise-the-same-but-unnecessarily-larger iPhone 6, even fans had begun to scoff. Parody videos for iPhone 5 had already mocked Apple's obsession with change with titles like "A Taller Change." Apple's own slogan for the 2014 line seemed almost like self-parody: "Bigger than bigger." Some have lamented the recent salvos in Apple's product arsenal, blaming CEO Tim Cook for betraying the company's commitment to the "revolutionary" ideals Steve Jobs seemed to embody. Even *The Onion* weighed in on the matter: "Apple Unveils Panicked Man with No Ideas." But Apple's transition from computers to clothier began long before Jobs's death—he just managed to avoid its consequences by establishing himself as a legend. The most impactful and lasting revolutions don't fetishize revolution itself but establish a new regime that lasts over time.

That's the legacy of the Apple II (personal computing), the Macintosh (computing for everybody), the iPod (music in your pocket) and the iPhone (connected computing, everywhere). We can't handle seasonal revolutions, even if it were possible to produce meaningful upheaval that rapidly. Just think of how we relate to Apple's laptop products: we treat them as necessities and ponder when to upgrade based on the urgency of our needs as regulated by the appeal of an incrementally improved model. The personal computer was once a revolutionary device, but now it's just a device. So too the iPhone, hereby transitioned from ingenious novelty to ordinary instrument in a little more than half a decade. Apple now deals in haute couture, not in high tech. Planned obsolescence has become design démodé.

5

The Cigarette of This Century

IN JANUARY 1995, a year and a half before Hotmail launched the world's first web-based email service, a landmark California law banning smoking in most public places went into effect. Back then, smoking was already on the decline, especially in California, but it was probably still more common than having an email account.

The change was most immediately noticeable in restaurants. No longer would a host or hostess ask "smoking or non-?" before seating you. It sounds silly today—most Americans bristle at the idea of smoking while eating, and many restaurants in states without explicit bans have chosen to prohibit smoking for social rather than legal reasons. Smokers are still around, of course, but now they excuse themselves to the courtyard or the alley, where they gather in groups like outcasts. In fact, they *are* outcasts, forced to commune with their habit and one another in private.

It used to be different. At smoking's peak in 1965, over 40 percent of the U.S. population lit up, compared to less than half that figure today. The rise of cigarette smoking took less time to evolve than it has to decline. By the turn of the twentieth century, the cigarette's small size and cheap cost made it readily available to most industrial populations. And thanks to milder tobaccos, its smoke could be inhaled more readily, making smoking a more comfortable and pleasurable affair. The cigarette is a technology, after all, subject to the same forces of innovation, adoption, and decline as the personal computer or the mobile phone. And as a technology, the cigarette offers utility beyond its intended purpose as a nicotine delivery apparatus. As Marshall McLuhan observed, it enhances a sense of poise and calm by giving the smoker a prop, reducing social awkwardness. It retrieves tribal practices of ritual and security and obsolesces loneliness by giving everyone something in common to do, such as asking for a light.

Five short years after California banned smoking in restaurants, connectivity seemed essential, and more and more work got done by email. The technology services company I worked for at the time bought me a BlackBerry 957, the taller version of Research in Motion's (RIM) pager-shaped wireless email device. Back then, a BlackBerry could read email or navigate to WAP websites, but it didn't work as a phone. It was summer 2000, a few months into the catastrophic end of the dot-com boom.

Mobile telephony was still nascent in 2000, and many people bought a cell phone just in case of emergencies. The business uses of mobile phones were slightly less melodramatic, but not much: the office wouldn't call for just anything, particularly after hours. Years later, personal uses of mobile phones have become more like workplace uses: call only if you have to. But the BlackBerry felt like something truly new. Being able to read and send email instantly, from anywhere, offered a whole different experience of work. For the first time, I could be reached anywhere in service of the most mundane of questions or requests.

I remember the first day I had the BlackBerry, hearing it buzz with new email notifications, sending a deep hum through the kitchen counter atop which it sat; at night, the blinking red light serving as a silent notification in the darkness on the nightstand; eventually—and it didn't take long—waking up at 2:00 a.m. to check it or, at the very least, picking it up first thing in the morning, before coffee, before even slipping on slippers.

At our Christmas party that year, an already dour affair thanks to the collapsing economy, my spouse and those of two of the other executives who'd been deemed important enough to warrant BlackBerry service complained about our compulsive habit. "Does he check it at night too?" "And at dinner. I hate it." "Mine uses it in the car, when he's at red lights or stuck on the freeway. Can you even imagine?" We knew they were annoyed, but we felt persecuted anyway. "Honey, this is *work*."

Today, all our wives and husbands have BlackBerries or iPhones or Galaxies or whatever—the progeny of those original 950 and 957 models that put data in our pockets. Now we all check email (or Twitter, or Facebook, or Instagram, or . . .) compulsively at the dinner table, or the traffic light. Now we all stow our devices on the nightstand before bed and check them first thing in the morning. We all do. It's not abnormal, and it's not just for business. It's just what people do. Like smoking in 1965, it's just life.

For years now, omens of RIM's possible demise have lingered in the air like stale cigarette smoke. How, some ask, could such a powerful and prescient company fall so hard, ceding their legacy to sector "upstarts" like Apple and Google? And indeed, the company may not survive the rise of its competitors. But calling BlackBerry a failure is like calling Lucky Strike a failure. Not just for its brand recognition and eponymy, but even more so for the fact that its products set up a chain reaction that has changed social behavior in a way we still don't fully understand—just as our parents and grandparents didn't fully understand the cigarette in the 1960s.

For McLuhan, when pushed to the limits of its powers, the cigarette flips into a nervous tic, an addiction. Perhaps the best way to grasp BlackBerry's legacy is by imagining a hypothetical future, fifty years hence, when compulsive Internet-connected personal devices overheat and reverse into their opposite. It's certainly possible to accuse smartphones of such a curse already, even if we never find as certain a detrimental effect as lung cancer was to cigarettes. We've already started to regulate texting while driving, after all.

But even absent an excuse grounded in public health and welfare, it is not unfathomable to imagine a prospective society that finds the tic itself to be as abhorrent and vile as today's culture does cigarettes. In that putative future, smartphone users would be relegated to special rooms in airports, where passersby would shake their heads disapprovingly at the gray faces lit from below by their tiny, blue screens. The father or mother who pulls a phone from a pocket at dinner would feel knowing shame, followed by the relief of new data. Crotchety former hipsters would gather outside the entryways of public buildings, tapping out tomorrow's relics of tweets or tumblrs while twenty-somethings pass by, oblivious.

Apple (and Google's Android, but via Apple's own reflection) has assumed the mantle of portable computing once held by BlackBerry. And though we may feel that such an office mostly entails how we work and play on our mobile devices, in the long run it matters very little which apps we run or which social networks we upload to from our smartphones. It's far more important that we carry them, that we look at them. That we *need* to look at them, such that we make excuses to do so.

Even in the heyday of the cigarette, children and teenagers were protected from them. They were a known sin, but they were a sin of adulthood. Sneaking a smoke was a surreptitious ritual of youth as much as a rite of passage. Even before the cigarette's status as carcinogen was widely known and accepted, something about them remained unseemly. Dirty, smelly, dark, dangerous. Perhaps the fact that cigarettes are literally *on fire* offered enough cover to help adults cover over the latent ignominy of using them—even when everyone did. And over time, the knowledge that smoking cigarettes would eventually kill you built into them a baseline mortification, an undeniable danger and imprudence. "I'm trying to quit," one could always rationalize between drags.

No equivalent indignity exists for today's smokes. Teens and children are encouraged to own and use smartphones. The iPod replaced the boom box or the video game console as the ultimate treasure to find under the Christmas tree. Even babies have iDevices now, thanks to special shock-and-drool-proof cases manufactured explicitly for them. To stare down a screen is just what we do. Everyone's pockets itch at the dinner table, as so many possibilities buzz anonymously under denim.

Now the shame comes in recognizing the absence of shame. As one's children grow into teenagers, as one can no longer deny them devices but might even justify their utility as communication tools, a stupid, aluminum-and-glass version of that trite Harry Chapin "Cat's in the Cradle" realization wafts up like the smoke it replaces: how can I tell my kid to put the phone away at the table or on the sofa, when I won't do so either? Without appeal to the immediate safety or longevity or financial burden that used to excuse the hypocrisy of adult smokers discouraging youths from adopting the habit, we can all sink into the tasteless, odorless sin of pocketable data.

It took fifty years for computers to move from office basements to handbags, and scarcely five more for them to enter our pockets. Now we take them everywhere. Laptops, tablets, smartphones: they are always on hand and, thanks to their portability, always at the ready. Even worse, they're always connected, and the boundless potential of a hypothetical interaction is always better than the specific reality of one actually taking place.

But even despite its ubiquity, we still itch with anxiety for having allowed computer-mediated interactions to eclipse face-to-face ones. Most often, detractors make appeals to etiquette and tradition as a salve for our newfound data habit. Isn't it rude to turn our attention away from people right in front of us?

It's a weak argument because you already know the answer, and you don't care. *Of course* it's rude to disrupt one conversation just in case another one might be more interesting. Obvious exceptions exist (family emergencies, urgent requests from a superior), but they rarely occur anyway. To ask if task switching to your smartphone is rude is to ask the wrong question. Instead, we should wonder why we seem so willing to adopt this particular kind of discourtesy. Some might answer that we haven't done so willingly, that we're compelled, even addicted to our gadgets and the services they deliver.

But compulsion isn't the whole story, either, just as it never was with cigarettes. The truth is that we secretly want to be rude. Rudeness is a sign of success, of power, of poise, of calm. Think of a figure who would willingly turn away from a conversation to take a call, who would show up late without apology, who would maintain total contingency in his affairs just in case something more important comes along.

It's none other than the corporate executive, who also happens to be the early adopter of the mobile phone and the BlackBerry that presaged today's connected devices. The executive always holds time in reserve, because he sees his time (or hers, but mostly his) as more precious than yours.

"I'm sorry, I have to take this" is less a statement of deference than it is one of authority: "I am important enough to snub you."

For better or worse, the businessman is the hero of contemporary culture. Our hero is no longer the rock star or the pro ballplayer or the actor but rather the wealthy Silicon Valley entrepreneur. It's no surprise that his manner would win out over Miss Manners in the public imagination. We rarely admit it, but we all want to be important, yet most of us aren't. Smartphones let us simulate that importance, replacing boardroom urgency with household triviality. And even though they seem like populist devices, smartphones can never fully shed their origins as rapacious instruments of executive grandstanding. There will always be something rude about smartphone use, because smartphones allow us all to play the role of a cultural paragon we didn't choose, one we may even despise, but one whose influence we can't disavow. Rather than blackening our lungs like yesteryear's handheld devices, today's blacken our hearts.

The point is not whether technologies like smartphones actually make us more or less connected to one another—that's a cheap, pat question whose answer is best left to trade books and TED talks. The point is that technologies like the BlackBerry and its progeny change our social fabric in ways that we often cannot see, and therefore cannot fully reason about. McLuhan argued that technologies can never be fully grasped in the present, but only after we establish some distance from them. Today, we lament the fall of RIM as if it were an athlete whose prodigious career was cut short by hubris. But perhaps the truth is even weirder than that.

Ruined or not, BlackBerry has left us with the most distinctive social tic since cigarettes, which Apple made palatable through the low-tar's design equivalent, Bauhaus modernism. And cigarettes may be deadly and disgusting, but they're cool and chic too. Pulling down an interface to refresh an app isn't all that different from taking a drag: the sensuous richness of the idea of new information at any moment, the egomania of feeling justified in always grasping at it, and the frothing, blooming world that spins unseen while we fondle our devices in search of something else.

6

Hyperemployment

IN 1930, the economist John Maynard Keynes famously argued that by the time a century had passed, developed societies would be able to replace work with leisure thanks to widespread wealth and surplus. "We shall do more things for ourselves than is usual with the rich to-day," he wrote, "only too glad to have small duties and tasks and routines." Eighty years hence, it's hard to find a moment in the day not filled with a duty or task or routine. If anything, it would seem that work has overtaken leisure almost entirely. We work increasingly hard for increasingly little, only to come home to catch up on the work we can't manage to work on at work.

Take email. A friend recently posed a question on Facebook: "Remember when email was fun?" It's hard to think back that far. On Prodigy, maybe, or with UNIX mail or Elm or Pine via telnet. Email was silly then, a trifle. A leisure activity out of Keynes's macroeconomic tomorrowland. It was full of excess, a thing done because it could be rather than because it had to be. The worst part of email was forwarded jokes, and even those seem charming in retrospect. Even junk mail is endearing when it's novel.

Now, email is a pot constantly boiling over. Like King Sisyphus pushing his boulder, we read, respond, delete, delete, delete, only to find that even more messages have arrived while we were pruning. A whole time management industry has erupted around email, urging us to check only once or twice a day, to avoid checking email first thing in the morning, and so forth. Even if such techniques work, the idea that managing the communication for a job now requires its own self-help literature reeks of a foul new anguish.

If you're like many people, you've started using your smartphone as an alarm clock. Now it's the first thing you see and hear in the morning. And touch, before your spouse or your crusty eyes. Then the ritual begins. Overnight, twenty or forty new emails: spam, solicitations, invitations, or requests from those whose days pass during your nights, mailing list reminders, bill pay notices. A quick triage, only to be undone while you shower and breakfast.

Email and online services have provided a way for employees to outsource work to one another. Whether you're planning a meeting with an online poll, requesting an expense report submission to an enterprise resource planning (ERP) system, asking that a colleague contribute to a shared Google Doc, or just forwarding on a notice that "might be of interest," jobs that previously would have been handled by specialized roles have now been distributed to everyone in an organization.

No matter what job you have, you probably have countless other jobs as well. Marketing and public communications were once centralized; now every division needs a social media presence, and maybe even a website to develop and manage. Thanks to Oracle and SAP, everyone is a part-time accountant and procurement specialist. Thanks to Oracle and Google Analytics, everyone is a part-time analyst.

And email has become the circulatory system along which internal outsourcing flows. Sending an email is easy and cheap, and emails create obligation on the part of a recipient without any prior agreement. In some cases, that obligation is bureaucratic, meant to drive productivity and reduce costs. "Self-service" software automation systems like these are nothing new—SAP's ERP software has been around since the 1970s. But since the 2000s, such systems can notify and enforce compliance via email requests and nags. In other cases, email acts as a giant human shield, a white-collar Strategic Defense Initiative. The worker who emails enjoys both assignment and excuse all at once. "Didn't you get my email?"

The despair of email has long left the workplace. Not just by infecting our evenings and weekends via Outlook web access and BlackBerry and iPhone, although it has certainly done that. Now we also run the email gauntlet with everyone. The ballet school's schedule updates (always received too late, but "didn't you get the email?"); the Scout troop announcements; the daily deals website notices; the PR distribution list you somehow got on after attending that conference; the insurance notification, informing you that your new coverage cards are available for self-service printing (you went paperless, yes?); and the email password reset notice that finally trickles in twelve hours later, because you forgot your insurance website password since a year ago. And so on.

It's easy to see email as unwelcome obligation, but too rarely do we take that obligation to its logical if obvious conclusion:

those obligations are increasingly akin to another job—or better, *many* other jobs. For those of us lucky enough to be employed, we're really *hyperemployed*—committed to our usual jobs and many other jobs as well. It goes without saying that we're not being paid for all these jobs, but pay is almost beside the point, because the real cost of hyperemployment is *time*. We are doing all those things others aren't doing instead of all the things we are competent at doing. And if we fail to do them, whether through active resistance or simple overwhelm, we alone suffer for it: the schedules don't get made, the paperwork doesn't get mailed, the proposals don't get printed, and on and on.

But the deluge doesn't stop with email, and hyperemployment extends even to the unemployed, thanks to our tacit agreement to work for so many Silicon Valley technology companies.

Increasingly, online life in general overwhelms. The endless, constant flow of email, notifications, direct messages, favorites, invitations. After that daybreak email triage, so many other icons on your phone boast badges silently enumerating their demands. Facebook notifications. Twitter @-messages, direct messages. Tumblr followers, Instagram favorites, Vine comments. Elsewhere too: comments on your blog, on your YouTube channel. The Facebook page you manage for your neighborhood association or your animal rescue charity. New messages in the forums you frequent. Your Kickstarter campaign updates. Your Etsy shop. Your eBay watch list. And then, of course, more email. Always more email.

Email is the plumbing of hyperemployment. Not only

do automated systems notify and direct us via email but we direct and regulate one another through email. But even beyond its function as infrastructure, email also has a disciplinary function. The content of email almost doesn't matter. Its primary function is to reproduce itself in enough volume to create anxiety and confusion. The constant flow of new email produces an endless supply of potential work. Even figuring out whether there is really any "actionable" effort in the endless stream of emails requires viewing, sorting, parsing, even before one can begin conducting the effort needed to act and respond.

We have become accustomed to using the term *precarity* to describe the condition whereby employment itself is unstable or insecure. But even within the increasingly precarious jobs, the work itself has become precarious too. Email is a mascot for this sensation. At every moment of the workday—and on into the evening and the night, thanks to smartphones—we face the possibility that some request or demand, reasonable or not, might be awaiting us.

Often, we cast these new obligations either as compulsions (the addictive, possibly dangerous draw of online life) or as necessities (the importance of digital contact and an "online brand" in the information economy). But what if we're mistaken, and both tendencies are really just symptoms of hyperemployment? We are now competing with ourselves for our own attention.

When critics engage with the demands of online services via labor, they often cite exploitation as a simple explanation. It's a sentiment that even has its own aphorism: "If you're not paying for the product, you are the product." The idea is that all the information you provide to Google and Facebook, all the content you create for Tumblr and Instagram, enables the primary business of such companies, which amounts to aggregating and reselling your data or access to it. In addition to the revenues extracted from ad sales, tech companies like YouTube and Instagram also managed to leverage the speculative value of your data-and-attention into billion-dollar buyouts. Tech companies are using you, and they're giving precious little back in return.

While often true, this phenomenon is not fundamentally new to online life. We get network television for free in exchange for the attention we devote to ads that interrupt our shows. We receive "discounts" on grocery store staples in exchange for allowing Kroger or Safeway to aggregate and sell our shopping data. Meanwhile, the companies we *do* pay directly as customers often treat us with disregard at best, abuse at worst (just think about your cable provider or your bank). Of course, we shouldn't just accept online commercial exploitation just because exploitation in general has been around for ages. Rather, we should acknowledge that exploitation only partly explains today's anxiety with online services.

Hyperemployment offers a subtly different way to characterize all the tiny effort we contribute to Facebook and Instagram and the like. It's not just that we've been duped into contributing free value to technology companies (although that's also true) but that we've tacitly agreed to work unpaid jobs for all these companies. And even calling them "unpaid" is slightly unfair, because we do get something back from these services, even if they often take more than they give.

Rather than just being exploited or duped, we've been hyper-employed. We do tiny bits of work for Google, for Tumblr, for Twitter, all day and every day.

Today, everyone's a hustler. But now we're not even just hustling for ourselves or our bosses but for so many other, unseen bosses. For accounts payable and for marketing; for the Girl Scouts and the Youth Choir; for Facebook and for Google; for our friends via their Kickstarters and their Etsy shops; for Twitter, whose initial public offering converted years of tiny, aggregated work acts into seventy-eight dollars of fungible value per user.

Even if there is more than a modicum of exploitation at work in the hyperemployment economy, the despair and overwhelm of online life don't derive from that exploitation—not directly anyway. Rather, it's a type of exhaustion cut of the same sort that afflicts the *underemployed* as well, like the single mother working two part-time service jobs with no benefits or the PhD working three contingent teaching gigs at three different regional colleges to scrape together a still insufficient income. The economic impact of hyperemployment is obviously different from that of underemployment, but some of the same emotional toll imbues both: a sense of inundation, of being trounced by demands whose completion yields only their continuance, and a feeling of resignation that no other scenario is likely or even possible. The only difference between the despair of hyperemployment and that of un- or underemployment is that the latter at least acknowledges itself as a substandard condition, whereas the former celebrates the hyperemployed's purported freedom to "share" and "connect," to do business more easily and effectively by doing jobs once left for others' competence and compensation, from the convenience of your car or toilet.

Staring down the barrel of Keynes's 2030 target for the arrival of universal leisure, economists have often considered why the economist seems to have been so wrong. The inflation of relative needs is one explanation—the arms race for better and more stuff and status. The ever-increasing wealth gap, on the rise since the anti-Keynes, supply-side 1980s, is another. But what if Keynes was right, too, in a way. Even if productivity has increased mostly to the benefit of the wealthy, hasn't *everyone* gained enormous leisure, but by replacing recreation with work rather than work with recreation? This new work doesn't even require employment; the destitute and unemployed hyperemployed are just as common as the affluent and retired hyperemployed. Perversely, it is only then, at the labor equivalent of the techno-anarchist's singularity, that the malaise of hyperemployment can cease. Then all time will become work time, and we will not have any memory of leisure to distract us.

7

Two Elegies for Apple

ONE

iPhones are manufactured with planned obsolescence built in: processors and RAM allocations that can't keep up with operating system upgrades purposely designed not to account for earlier models. Apple makes too much of its profits from hardware sales, so handsets have become akin to fashion seasons, because couture can justify rapid replacement in a way that mere electronic facility cannot.

Hardware upgrades entail power and capacity. The new activities made possible by new silicon. But there's another kind of planned obsolescence: that of degradation.

Thrice now, with three different iPhones many years apart in service, I've reached a point when the home button begins failing. The level of atrophy displayed in this singular haptic interface varies. My iPhone 4 button stopped working completely; on my iPhone 5, it merely behaves erratically. The degeneration mostly exhibits in the form of an overly eager Siri, like an elderly relative at a family gathering.

"What? What did you need?" With that shrill beep-beep you can't disable, the one that doesn't even respect the mute switch.

No, I wasn't talking to you, Siri. You can go back to sleep. But even that takes time. She has to settle back into the unseen background of the OS, as if creaking back into a plastic-covered davenport (that's what she'd call it).

It's come to be expected, like any degeneracy. Like someone might apologize for her elderly dog as she carts it down the stairs, now we apologize for our elderly smartphones, and to knowing, empathetic nods. A bum home button is just a sign of a device's inevitable end, a memento mori for our digital companions. "I know it's old for an iPhone," we might whisper, as if it can understand, like we might do for a Yorkie.

We say "my phone is dying" when it needs to be charged. "Sorry I didn't call; my phone died." But our phones also die for real. Apple sees to it. They count on it.

It's upsetting to be lured into personifying a smartphone. It's a burden we shouldn't have to face. A dull knife or a failing vacuum can't perform their jobs either, but at least they don't incite guilt or anger. Apple's decades-long project to make computer technology friendly and personable has been too successful. Maybe we'd be better off if we returned to the inhuman honesty of simple machinery.

TWO

Steve Jobs was a fascist. That's what everyone loved about him: he told us what *he* wanted, and he convinced us we are going to like it. And we did, and we do, not because he was right (despite popular opinion) but because it's so rare to get such definitive, brazen, abusive treatment in this era of lowest-common-denominator wishy-washiness. It doesn't matter if he was right because his design sense is so definitive that it outstripped truth in favor of legend.

In that sense, Jobs's departure from Apple's helm and, soon after, his death have to be seen in the same way as would the departure or deposition or death of a dictator, but in reverse, because Jobs himself was Apple's primary feature and value. Did Jobs successfully "download" his own authoritarianism into Apple writ large, such that it can continue into the future as a machine without figurehead? Even years later, it's hard to say. Though it's a metaphor rather than an analogy, most authoritarian political regimes are cults of personality, and in that respect, the golden era may be over. That's the reason for all the elegiac sentiments we saw in the press after the announcement of his resignation as CEO and then again after his death. It wasn't Jobs's untimely end everyone lamented but rather the end of his regime.

From the perspective of legacy, Jobs should have deployed nepotism and divine right, rearing one of his children as a successor. Perhaps he did, after a fashion, in his close friend Jony Ive, Apple's senior vice president of design, who survived the rule of business at Apple before Jobs's return to power in 1997. Fascism and modernism go hand in hand:

symmetry and simplicity, in the service of total unification of the population, toward the realization of its autarch's unyielding vision. Tim Cook may make the trains run on time, but the people don't want trains, they want cold, gray dirigibles slinking across the bright sky, glints of sunlight blinding them, so far below, so far below.

8

Can We Have Your Attention, Please?

GODVILLE IS A "ZERO-PLAYER" iPhone game. It's called that because, supposedly, play doesn't require a player but only the game. According to its creators, Godville "is a parody on everything from 'typical' MMO games with their tedious level ups, to internet memes and ordinary day to day things appealing to a wide audience."

A zero-player game (ZPG, the creators acronymize) is a big promise to keep. When I played Godville, I discovered that it offered a great deal of computer-generated detail about its goings on, all in the guise of the conventions of the traditional role-playing game. For example: "11:46 a.m.: The dying Radioactive Cockroach gave me 18 coins and brought me one step closer to world supremacy."

No matter though. Soon enough I discovered that it was necessary for me, the player, to intervene in the game after all by means of "god power." Small actions allowed me to influence my character's fate. It even sells gam`eplay "energy" in earnest via microtransactions! Aesthetically, it's a little

6

disappointing. A true ZPG wouldn't require any play at all, wouldn't it? But there's the rub, of course: a ZPG without gameplay is really just a novella or a short story. It's harder than it looks to game the very idea of an app.

iCapitalism offers another attempt at such a feat. It's an iOS game that critiques both capitalism and iOS games through a simple design. Like Godville, it attempts no gameplay; iCapitalism is driven entirely by microtransactions. When you make purchases in the game, your rank rises on the leaderboard. Players are allowed to post a message on the leaderboard, so the most free of wallet also get their messages heard, at least within the context of iCapitalism.

As casual mobile and online games move away from challenge and strategy toward the (equally valid) purpose of idle time wasting, it's worth reminding ourselves of the logical (if absurd) end point of such efforts: playing a game that isn't a game but just a stand-in for the results of playing one.

Or, it would have been, had anyone been allowed to not-play iCapitalism: as it had done with Molleindustria's Phone Story, Apple rejected the app during App Store review, the secretive and unpredictable process by which software gets "approved" for download and consumption on Apple's carefully controlled marketplace.

App rejections aren't uncommon, but iCapitalism's developers seemed confused by theirs. They noted in a blog post that they didn't use any undocumented APIs, a common reason for rejection. But Apple didn't reject the game because it did something dangerous; Apple rejected it because doing nothing is considered dangerous. Apple exercised its then-new policy to limit programs that don't offer much value (in its estimation). From the "App Store Review Guidelines" at the time of iCapitalism's failed release:

> We have over 250,000 apps in the App Store. We don't need any more Fart apps.
>
> If your app doesn't do something useful or provide some form of lasting entertainment, it may not be accepted.
>
> If your App looks like it was cobbled together in a few days, or you're trying to get your first practice App into the store to impress your friends, please brace yourself for rejection. We have lots of serious developers who don't want their quality Apps to be surrounded by amateur hour.

Beyond mere languor, Apple has also implied that the more an app charges (whether through initial purchase or in-app purchases), the more strenuous their review will become.

The problem is this: iCapitalism *does* do something useful *and* provides some form of lasting entertainment—precisely by not doing anything useful in a smart way. Apple's ironic blindness for irony on the App Store is legendary, but in this case I doubt the faceless review bureaucrats even realize that the joke's on them. Yet, for their part, the iCapitalism developers also degrade from sharp (if simplistic) commentary into all-too-familiar whining about Apple review policies. As if an app like iCapitalism isn't about app review as much as it is about capitalism.

These days, satire always risks becoming mere conceptual art. Mockery is increasingly indistinguishable from the subject it mocks. "Not the *Onion*," we type on Facebook when linking a story that inevitably incites the question. Today, all "content" is barely more than a parody of content, a clickbait trick to get you to look or to sign up, such that your hypothetical future value might be leveraged into speculative financial instrument.

The only difference between conceptual art and speculative finance is that people consider one a noble pursuit and the other a joke. The art world can thank itself for having brought about this attitude. In the heyday of conceptual art, it was sufficient artistic work simply to question that the work itself was the important part of the art. Conceptual artists were always dealing in derivatives of art, not in art itself. Marcel Duchamp's readymades (including his most famous work, *Fountain*, a urinal relocated to a gallery) were less critiques of art than they were art world derivatives, art trading in the very idea of the value of art. Soon enough, derivatives became a primary mode of art. What better way to draw attention to the process and context of art than simply to post instructions for making art as the art itself—such was conceptualist Sol LeWitt's strategy, one further developed by Robert Rauschenberg, Yoko Ono, Piero Manzoni, and others.

When Manzoni claimed to have encased his own feces in a box that he then exhibited, the effect was clear: it provoked certain questions in the viewer. Can shit be art? Does it matter if there's really shit in the box? Is art meant to represent anyway, or just to provoke? But there's a problem: conceptual art is precious and gimmicky. Like derivatives trading, it is inherently fragile and risky. And it has proliferated, overtaking almost all other forms of contemporary creativity. It's become the norm. So much art is conceptual nowadays, even work that doesn't deserve the name "art."

Today, conceptual art is everywhere, and nowhere more than in our computational media. What's that most famous of non-apps, iFart, but conceptual art? It poses questions like, what if your fancy new five hundred dollar iPhone were just a whoopee cushion? What is the minimum functionality possible in an app? Why is farting any less absurd and embarrassing than tweeting or receiving phone calls in public? Taken to its extreme, even the iPhone itself might qualify as conceptual art: one big attention derivative swap betting on your and my unwillingness or inability to put the thing down.

In its own backward, totally unaware way, when Apple refuses to publish software like iCapitalism, the company is struggling to accept its role in the ascendance of conceptual art, a form the company also clearly wants to despise. It's no longer sufficient to pose a question like "what if an app did nothing but ask you to spend money?" Instead, it ought to *get people to do nothing more than to spend money*, offering tiny, subtle peepholes through which to understand the difference between enjoyment and absurdity. Admittedly, this is much harder work than the conceptual artists of the twentieth century faced. Apple hopes not to facilitate the further rise of conceptual art *as art* but to endorse a derivatives bundle of speculation in creativity, finance, and attention.

If products like iCapitalism don't effectively characterize the logical conclusion of such thinking, what might fit the bill? Enter Yo, an app created by Israeli entrepreneur Or Arbel, reportedly in a mere eight hours' time. All it does is send the message "Yo" to an interlocutor. Arbel has raised one million dollars in angel investment, a fact that the Internet has responded to with reasonable astonishment ("Not the *Onion*," your friends may have written when linking to news of Yo's yodelers).

In essence, Yo is just a very simplified digital pager—like the kind doctors used to use, the sort BlackBerry adapted into the precursor to the smartphone. Re-creating the pager for the twenty-first century certainly exudes the musk of conceptual art, but it also surprisingly uncovers the attentional hook that start-ups like Yo and companies like Apple rely on to create speculative future value.

A pager—Yo included—poses one question and facilitates its answer: "Are you here?" That's all we want to know, anymore. Are you here, reading me? Reviewing my book? Liking or faving or retweeting me? It's what you want to know when you text your significant other or your child. Are you there? Is everything okay? Yes, yes, I'm here. All good. Okay.

Sometimes in stupidity we find a frankness, an honesty. This truth of contemporary communication practice is undeniable, yet we persist in using tools that exceed it. Natural language, even when condensed into textspeak. The meteoric rise of emoji. We often want to communicate, but even more often we simply want to *meta-communicate*, to possess the knowledge that an individual or group will acknowledge us.

Like most conceptual art, Yo is stupid. There's no other word for it. But fifty thousand people sent four million Yos between the app's launch on, uhm, April Fool's Day 2014 and the summer solstice of that year. But sometimes in stupidity we find a kind of frankness, an honesty. For his part,

Arbel has rather overstated the matter. "We like to call it context-based messaging," he told the *New York Times*. "You understand by the context what is being said."

This kind of fancy talk, combined with an influx of investment capital and the attendant expectations of billion-dollar valuations, rankles the everyman. It sounds like nonsense and duplicity: another tech buffoon trying to dupe the world into enough attention to yield a quick, profitable exit. And it is that, make no mistake. But there's something undeniably *true* about the underlying premise of Yo.

Not its story as a tech start-up, which is more of the usual. By spring, Arbel had taken his million dollars in venture capital and moved to San Francisco to work on Yo full-time. By early autumn its users had sent more than one hundred million Yos.

Rather, about the way constant, always-on, always-available communication devices and networks have amplified the function of meta-communication. We talk a lot about "content" today, our accidental nickname for anything that gets digitized and sent over electronic networks. But the truest, most fundamental type of content is simply attention. And what better summary of attention than "hello"—or "yo," if you must. When we talk online, mostly we say variants of that one thing: *Here I am*. Are you here? Yes, yes, I'm here. And these statements have just as much meaning when withheld: no, I'm not here, not for you at least, or not right now.

The problem with Yo isn't what makes it stupid—its attempt to formalize the meta-communication common to online life—but what makes it gross: the need to contain all human activity within the logics of tech start-ups. For the record, such grossness is isomorphic to that found in conceptual art (everything is art!) and financial speculation writ large (everything is financial instrument!).

But an inconvenient truth shows its face when we bundle conceptual art, finance, and technology: such a derivative social contract amplifies the belligerence of all three. Like Facebook Poke before it, Yo might send the wrong signal about the way we send signals. Despite its creator's insistence that Yo eliminates meaning in favor of context, it actually adopts a very particular and specific meaning. *Yo* is a dudebro's term. It's stocky and aggressive. It doesn't just say, "Here I am," it does so by thrusting its chest out at you. Just as Poke felt creepy—a bad, unwelcome touch—so Yo installs a similarly invasive subtext.

And speaking of that, one can't ignore the context of Yo's creation. Arbel is a young, white, male engineer financed by a group led by other white, male entrepreneurs—a club of Israeli business compatriots that one might not be wrong to call a fraternity. Meta-communicative though it may be, "yo" doesn't say "are you here" so much as it says "I expect something from you."

The need to *expect something* from every idea, even the stupid ones, to feel that they deserve attention, users, data, and, inevitably, payout—perhaps this is the greatest meta-communicative message of today's technology scene. And it might not be inaccurate to summarize that message with a singular, guttural "yo."

9

The End of the Hangup

"CAN I USE MY TELEPHONE TO CALL GRANDMA?" my daughter asks. She means the Western Electric model 500 we bought at an antiques store at her insistence—a curiosity that is now more household sculpture than communication appliance.

The model 500 is the most common telephone set ever made, issued by Bell Systems from the 1950s through their divestiture in 1984. A black, desktop phone with a heavy handset and an angled rotary dial face: it's iconic, the archetype of "telephone." Or at least it used to be.

The telephone jacks and lines in our prewar bungalow still work even if we use them rarely, preferring our mobile phones for daily calls. I plug in the model 500 and show her how to dial it: swish-whirrrrr, swish-whirr, swish-whirrrrrrrrrrr.

Halfway through the conversation, Grandma has disappeared. "I don't know what happened," my son reports. It turns out he had depressed the hook switch and closed the line. Today's expectations don't quite match a device designed for the 1950s. If modern user interaction designers had their way with the model 500, depressing the hook switch while a call was connected would probably prompt the caller: "Are you sure you want to disconnect the current call? Dial 1 for yes, 2 for no."

I help the kids call grandma back, and we all have a laugh about it. But the unfortunate encounter with the model 500 hook switch makes me realize: it's no longer possible to hang up a phone.

When I was a kid, we had a bright yellow, rotary Western Electric model 554, the wall-mountable companion to the 500 desk set. Before answering machines, caller ID, *69, and, eventually, smartphone address books allowed us to screen calls quickly, a ringing phone was a pressing matter. It could mean anything: a friend's invitation, a neighbor's request, a family emergency. You had to answer to find out. Telephones rang loud, too, with urgency and desperation. One simply did not ignore the telephone.

In the context of such gravity, the hangup had a clear and forceful meaning. It offered a way of ending a conversation prematurely, sternly, aggressively. Without saying anything, the hangup said something: we're done, go away.

My father took great pride in hanging up our model 554 phone violently when something went awry. An inbound wrong number dialed twice in a row or an unwelcome solicitor. Clang! The handset's solid mass crashed down on the hook, the bell assembly whimpering from the impact. The mechanical nature of telephones made hangups a material affair as much as a social one. A hangup is something your interlocutor could feel physically as much as emotionally, and something you couldn't downplay either. Like slamming a door or yelling at a child, hanging up a phone couldn't be subdued or hidden.

Unlike today's cellular network, the public switched telephone network was robust and centralized thanks to monopoly. Apart from flukes like my son depressing the hook switch, a disconnected landline call is almost unheard of. By contrast, it's not possible to hang up on someone via smartphone with deliberateness, because it's so much more likely that the network itself will disconnect of its own accord. Every call is tenuous, constantly at risk of failing as a result of system instability: spectrum auctions, tower optimizations, network traffic, and so forth. The infrastructure is too fragile to make hangups stand out as affairs of agency rather than of accident.

Today a true hangup—one you really meant to perform out of anger or frustration or exhaustion—is only temporary and one-sided even when it is successfully executed. Even during a heated exchange, your interlocutor will first assume something went wrong in the network, and you could easily pretend such a thing was true later if you wanted. Calls aren't ever really under our control anymore; they "drop" intransitively. The signal can be lost, the device's battery can deplete, the caller can accidentally bump the touch screen and end the call, the phone's operating system can crash. The mobile hangup never signals itself as such but remains shrouded in uncertainties.

The physical design of telephones has made the hangup impossible for the would-be hanger-up as well. The model 500 series telephone supports hangups as a function of its physical form. It comes in two parts, base and handset, offering something to hang up and something to hang it upon. Flip-style mobile phones were the last devices to offer a physical equivalent, the crisp, satisfying snap of the closing shell offering a reasonable parallel to the handset and hook.

Hanging up on someone is a physical act, a violent one even, one that produces its own pleasure by discharging acrimony. Like the model 500, the flip-phone supports hangups because its form is capable of resisting them—because it can survive the force a hangup delivers. Just try to hang up your iPhone. I don't mean just ending a call, but hanging up for real, as if you meant it. For a moment you might consider throwing the handset against a wall before remembering that you shelled out three, four, five hundred dollars or more for the device, a thing you cradle in a cozy as if it were a kitten or a newborn.

Everyone is a milquetoast when a smartphone is in his hand. Relenting, you might slide it across a table or a counter to signal your distress—with a necessary gentleness that belies true disgust.

By contrast, the model 500 handset acted as a proxy, a voodoo doll for your interlocutor as much as an audio route. The mobile handset is different: an extension of the self rather than an implement. To do violence to it amounts to self-harm rather than catharsis. In fact, it's barely possible even to hang up mobile calls in the ordinary sense, after their natural completion in typical circumstances. The solid handset of the Bell era may remain imprinted upon smartphone displays or buttons as skeuomorphic icons, but the device itself invites you simply to "end" the call, like one might end high tea. And even that isn't necessary. Unlike a conventional switched line, a mobile device won't remain on the grid absent a live connection. After a call, it's not uncommon simply to stow a smartphone without further interaction and wait for the other party's disconnection to terminate the call.

Lamenting the demise of hangups offers little more than crass nostalgia for an admittedly weird, anonymous aggression. It's pointless wistfulness, too, because the phone call itself has become an endangered species. Today we have replaced synchronous communication methods with asynchronous ones: email, text messaging, even instant messaging are means of dispatch for which reply is never guaranteed, nor perhaps even expected. Where the analog telephone sampled the voices of callers as they spoke, computer and smartphone communication systems sample larger temporal swaths of social behavior.

Today, we've traded in our hangups for our hang-ups. The social disruption we now give or get via mobile devices is not the belligerence of hanging up or having been hung up on but the neurosis of not having received a response. In place of the threat of disengagement in fixed-line switched analog telephony, we find a subtly different fear in cellular telephony and its digital cousins: that of disregard. In the past the telephone was most threatening when it cut someone off; today its greatest menace is to reveal that you were never really connected in the first place.

10
Future Ennui

AT THE START OF 2015, fewer than eight short years since the first launch of the iPhone, Apple was worth more than seven hundred billion dollars—more than the gross national product of Switzerland. Despite its origins as a computer company, this is a fortune built from smartphones more than laptops. Before 2007, smartphones were a curiosity, mostly an affectation of would-be executives carting Black-Berries and Treos in unfashionable belt holsters. Not even a decade ago, they were wild and feral. Today, smartphones are fully domesticated. Tigers made kittens, which we now pet ceaselessly. More than two-thirds of Americans own them, and they have become the primary form of computing.

But along with that domestication comes the inescapability of docility. Have you not accepted your smartphone's reign over you rather than lamenting it? Stroking our glass screens, Chihuahua-like, is just what we *do* now, even if it also feels sinful. The hope and promise of new computer technology have given way to the malaise of living with it.

Shifts in technology are also shifts in culture and custom. And these shifts have become more frequent and more rapid over time. Before 2007, one of the most substantial technological shifts in daily life was probably the World Wide Web, which was already commercialized by the mid-1990s and mainstream by 2000. Before that? The personal computer, perhaps, which took from about 1977 until 1993 or so to become a staple of both home and business life. First we computerized work, then we computerized home and social life, then we condensed and transferred that life to our pockets. With the Apple Watch, now the company wants to condense it even further and have you wear it on your wrist.

Change is exciting, but it can also be exhausting. And for the first time in a long time, reactions to the Apple Watch seem to underscore exhaustion as much as excitement. But even these skeptical replies question the watch's implementation rather than expressing lethargy at the prospect of living in the world it might bestow on us.

Some have accused Apple of failing to explain the purpose of its new wearable. The wristwatch connoisseur Benjamin Clymer calls it a "market leader in a category nobody asked for." Apple veteran Ben Thompson rejoins Cook for failing to explain "why the Apple Watch existed, or what need it is supposed to fill." Felix Salmon agrees, observing that Apple "has always been the company which makes products for real people, rather than gadgets for geeks," before lamenting that the Apple Watch falls into the latter category.

"Apple *hasn't solved* the basic smartwatch dilemma," Salmon writes. But the dilemma he's worried about proves to be a banal detail: "Smart watches use up far more energy than dumb watches." He later admits that Apple might solve the battery and heft problems in a couple generations, but

"I'm not holding my breath." Salmon reacts to the Apple Watch's design and engineering failings rather than lamenting the more mundane afflictions of being subjected to wrist-sized emails in addition to desktop- and pocket-sized ones. We're rearranging icons on the *Titanic*.

After the Apple keynote, the *Onion* joked about the real product Apple had unveiled—a "brief, fleeting moment of excitement." But like so much satire these days, it's not really a joke. As Dan Frommer recently suggested, the Apple keynote is no less a product than are its phones and tablets. Apple is in the business of introducing big things as much as it is in the business of designing, manufacturing, distributing, and supporting them. In part, it has to be: Apple's massive valuation, revenues, and past successes have only increased the street's expectations for the company. In a world of so-called disruptive innovation, a company like Apple is expected to manufacture market-defining hit after hit.

Indeed, business is another context we often use to avoid engaging with our technological weariness. We talk about how Apple's CEO Tim Cook must steer the tech giant into new waters—such as wearables—to ensure a fresh supply of desire, customers, and revenue. But the exigency of big business has an impact on our ordinary lives. It's easy to cite the negative effects of a business environment focused on quarterly profits above all else, including maintaining job stability and paying into the federal or municipal tax base. In the case of Apple, something else is going on, too. In addition to being an economic burden, the urgency of technological innovation has become so habitual that we have become resigned to it. Wearables might not be perfect yet, we conclude, but they will happen. They already have.

I'm less interested in accepting wearables given the right technological conditions as I am prospectively exhausted at the idea of dealing with that future's existence. Just think about it. All those people staring at their watches in the parking structure, in the elevator. Tapping and stroking them, nearly spilling their coffee as they swivel their hands to spin the watch's tiny crown control.

A whole new tech cliché convention: the zoned-out smartwatch early adopter staring into his outstretched arm, like an inert judoka at the ready. The inevitable thinkpieces turned nonfiction trade books about "wrist shrift" or some similarly punsome quip on the promise-and-danger of wearables.

The variegated buzzes of so many variable "haptic engine" vibrations, sending notices of emails arriving from a boss or a spammer or obscene images received from a Facebook friend. The terrible battery life Salmon worries about, and the necessity of purchasing a new, expensive wristwatch every couple years, along with an equally costly smartphone with which to mate it.

The emergence of a new, laborious media creation and consumption ecosystem built for glancing. The rise of the "glancicle," which will replace the listicle. The PR emails and the b2b advertisements and the business consulting conference promotions all asking, "Is your brand glance-aware?"

These are mundane future grievances, but they are also likely ones. Unlike those of its competitor Google, with its eyeglass wearables and delivery drones and autonomous cars, Apple's products are reasonable and expected—prosaic even, despite their refined design. Google's future is truly science fictional, whereas Apple's is mostly foreseeable. You can imagine wearing Apple Watch, in no small part because you remember thinking that you could imagine carrying Apple's iPhone—and then you did, and now you always do.

Technology moves fast, but its speed now slows us down. A torpor has descended, the weariness of having lived this change before—or one similar enough, anyway—and all too recently. The future isn't even here yet, and it's already exhausted us in advance.

It's a far cry from "future shock," Alvin Toffler's 1970 term for the postindustrial sensation that too much change happens in too short a time. Where once the loss of familiar institutions and practices produced a shock, now it produces something more tepid and routine. The planned obsolescence that coaxes us to replace our iPhone 5 with an iPhone 6 is no longer disquieting but just expected. *I have to have one* has become *Of course I'll get one*. The idea that we might willingly reinvent social practice around wristwatch computers less than a decade after reforming it for smartphones is no longer surprising but predictable. We've heard this story before; we know how it ends.

Future shock is over. Apple Watch reveals that we suffer a new affliction: *future ennui*. The excitement of a novel technology (or anything, really) has been replaced—or at least dampened—by the anguish of knowing its future burden. This listlessness might yet prove even worse than blind boosterism or cynical naysaying. Where the trauma of future shock could at least light a fire under its sufferers, future ennui exudes the viscous languor of indifferent acceptance. It doesn't really matter that the Apple Watch doesn't seem necessary, no more than the iPhone once didn't too. Increasingly, change is not revolutionary, to use a word Apple has made banal, but presaged.

Our lassitude will probably be great for the companies like Apple that have worn us down with the constancy of their pestering. The poet Charles Baudelaire called ennui the worst sin, the one that could "swallow the world in a yawn." As Apple Watch leads the suppuration of a new era of wearables, who has energy left to object? Who has the leisure for revolution, as we keep up with our social media timelines and emails and home thermostats and heart monitors?

When one is enervated by future ennui, there's no vigor left even to ask if this future is one we even want. And even if we ask, lethargy will likely curtail our answers. No matter, though: soon enough, only a wrist's glance worth of ideas will matter anyway. And at that point, even this short book's worth of reflections on technology will be too much to bear, incompatible with our newfound obsession with wrist-sizing ideas. I'm sure I'll adapt, like you will. Living with Apple means marching ever forward, through its aluminum- and glass-lined streets and into the warm, selfsame glow of the future.

Notes

2. WHAT IS AN APP?

"The primary thing that Apple did . . ."
Steven An, comment on "Opinion: The Mac App Store and the PC Gamepocalypse," *Gamasutra*, January 10, 2011, http://www .gamasutra.com/view/news/32352/Opinion_The_Mac_App_ Store_And_The_PC_Gamepocalypse.php#comment82275.

3. PASCAL SPOKEN HERE

"Applications must be originally written in Objective-C . . ."
From the iPhone OS 4 SDK, section 3.3.1. Long since replaced by more recent versions, but for commentary and citation, see John Gruber, "New iPhone Developer Agreement Bans the Use of Adobe's Flash-to-iPhone Compiler," *Daring Fireball*, April 8, 2010, http://daringfireball.net/2010/04/ iphone_agreement_bans_flash_compiler.

5. THE CIGARETTE OF THIS CENTURY

"At smoking's peak in 1965, over 40 percent of the U.S. population lit up . . ."
Centers for Disease Control and Prevention (CDC), "Trends in Current Cigarette Smoking among High School Students

and Adults, United States, 1965–2011," http://www.cdc.gov/tobacco/data_statistics/tables/trends/cig_smoking/.

6. HYPEREMPLOYMENT

"In 1930, the economist John Maynard Keynes famously argued . . ."
John Maynard Keynes, *Essays in Persuasion* (New York: W. W. Norton, 1963), 358–73.

8. CAN WE HAVE YOUR ATTENTION, PLEASE?

"Godville 'is a parody on everything from "typical" MMO games with their tedious level ups . . .'"
From the Godville iTunes App Store description, http://itunes.apple.com/app/id353421868?mt=8.

"They noted in a blog post . . ."
"iRejected! How Apple Took Nine Weeks to Arbitrarily Reject Our App," *Forumwarz* (blog), February 1, 2011, http://blog.forumwarz.com/2011/02/01/irejected-how-apple-took-nine-weeks-to-arbitrarily-reject-our-app/.

"From the 'App Store Review Guidelines' at the time of iCapitalism's failed release . . ."
Jennifer Valentino-Devries, "Apple's Review Guidelines: 'We Don't Need Any More Fart Apps,'" *Wall Street Journal*, September 9, 2010, http://blogs.wsj.com/digits/2010/09/09/apples-review-guidelines-we-dont-need-any-more-fart-apps/.

"But fifty thousand people sent four million Yos . . ."
Jordan Crook, "Yo," *TechCrunch*, June 18, 2014, http://techcrunch.com/2014/06/18/yo-yo/.

"We like to call it context-based messaging . . ."
William Alden and Sydney Ember, "Messaging App Gets Peo-

ple Talking with One Word: Yo," *New York Times*, June 18, 2014, http://dealbook.nytimes.com//2014/06/18/with-single -word-yo-messaging-app-gets-people-talking/.

"... more than one hundred million Yos ..."
Seth Fiegerman, "Yo App Users Have Sent More Than 100 Million Yos," *Mashable*, September 5, 2014, http://mashable. com/2014/09/05/yo-100-million/.

10. FUTURE ENNUI

"... Apple was worth more than seven hundred billion dollars ..."
Verne Kopytoff, "Apple: The First $700 Billion Company," *Fortune*, February 10, 2015, http://fortune.com/2015/02/10/ apple-the-first-700-billion-company/.

"The wristwatch connoisseur Benjamin Clymer calls it a 'market leader in a category nobody asked for.'"
Benjamin Clymer, "A Watch Guy's Thoughts on the Apple Watch after Seeing It in the Metal," *Hodinkee*, September 7, 2014, http://www.hodinkee.com/blog/hodinkee-apple-watch-review.

"Felix Salmon agrees ..."
Felix Salmon, "Apple Hasn't Solved the Smart Watch Dilemma," *Medium*, September 9, 2014, https://medium.com/@felixsalmon/ apple-hasnt-solved-the-smart-watch-dilemma-5c8b61ca97f0.

"As Dan Frommer recently suggested, the Apple keynote is no less a product ..."
Dan Frommer, "The Hidden Structure of the Apple Keynote," *Quartz*, September 8, 2014, http://qz.com/261181/the -hidden-structure-of-the-apple-keynote/.

"It's a far cry from 'future shock,' Alvin Toffler's 1970 term ..."
Alvin Toffler, *Future Shock* (New York: Random House, 1970).

Ian Bogost is Ivan Allen College Distinguished Chair in Media Studies and professor of interactive computing at Georgia Institute of Technology, where he also holds an appointment in the Scheller College of Business. His books include *How to Do Things with Videogames* (Minnesota, 2011) and *Alien Phenomenology, or What It's Like to Be a Thing* (Minnesota, 2012).